PHONICS BLENDS

Written by **Lillian Duggan**

Illustrated by **Maru Jara**

FlashKids™

A Division of Barnes & Noble Publishing

This book belongs to

_____

Spark Educational Publishing
A Division of Barnes & Noble Publishing
120 Fifth Avenue
New York, NY 10011

ISBN 1-4114-0010-0

Please submit changes or report errors to _www.sparknotes.com/errors_

Printed and bound in China

For more information, please visit _www.flashkidsbooks.com_

Dear Parent,

Learning consonant sounds is an important part of reading. This book will help your child identify the sounds of consonant blends. The book includes matching activities and crossword puzzles to give your child lots of practice distinguishing the different consonant blends. To get the most from the activities included in this book, follow these simple steps:

- Find a comfortable place where you and your child can work quietly together.
- Encourage your child to go at his or her own pace.
- Help your child sound out the letters and identify the pictures.
- Offer lots of praise and support.
- Let your child reward his or her work with the included stickers.
- Most of all, remember that learning should be fun! Take time to look at the pictures, laugh at the funny characters, and enjoy this special time spent together.

What a Scare!

Blend the **s** and **c** sounds to say the beginning sound in **scare**. Circle the pictures that begin with the same sound as **scare**.

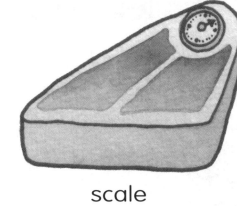

scale

cape

scarf

scarecrow

car

Slow as a Slug

Blend the **s** and **l** sounds to say the beginning sound in **slow** and **slug**. Circle the pictures that begin with the same sound as **slow** and **slug**.

slide

seed

clown

flag

sled

Slim Tim

Read the sentences. Draw a line from
each sentence to its matching picture.

Slim Tim slides on a sled.

Slim Tim sleeps on a scale.

Slim Tim eats a slice of cake.

Just a Small Fall

Blend the **s** and **m** sounds to say the beginning sound in **small**. Circle the pictures that begin with the same sound as **small**.

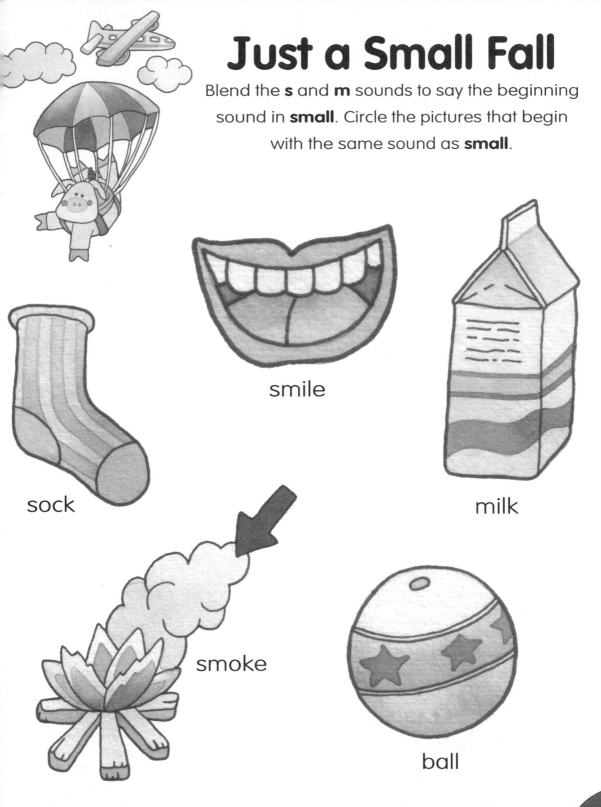

smile

milk

sock

smoke

ball

Crossword Fun

Match the pictures to the words in the list. Fill in the puzzle.

slide smile scale sleep smell

Across

2.

3.

4.

Down

1.

3.

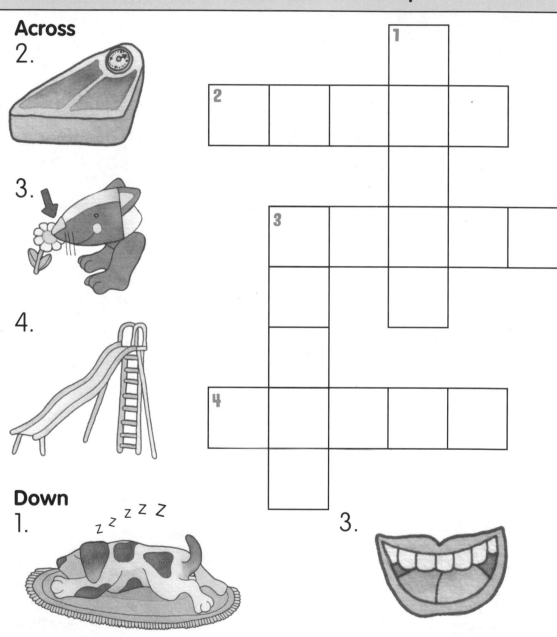

Don't Skid, Skip!

Blend the **s** and **k** sounds to say the beginning sound in **skid** and **Skip**. Circle the pictures that begin with the same sound as **skid** and **Skip**.

skunk

cake

skirt

skate

shirt

Skip's Day

Read the sentences. Draw a line from each sentence to its matching picture.

Skip smiles.

Skip skates.

Skip smells smoke!

Please, Not Another Snore!

Blend the **s** and **n** sounds to say the beginning sound in **snore**.

Circle the pictures that begin with the same sound as **snore**.

nail

sail

snow

snail

snake

Crossword Fun

Match the pictures to the words in the list. Fill in the puzzle.

snap skin skate slice snake

Across

2.

3.

Down

1.

2.

3.

Sparky in Space

Blend the **s** and **p** sounds to say the beginning sound in **Sparky** and **space**. Circle the pictures that begin with the same sound as **Sparky** and **space**.

snail

spider

sun

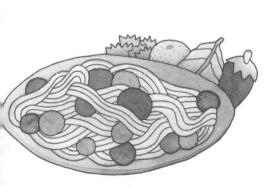

spaghetti

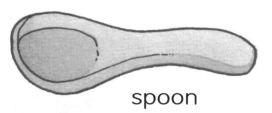

spoon

Snake and Snail Spin

Read the sentences. Draw a line from
each sentence to its matching picture.

A snake and a snail spin with speed.

A spider makes a splash.

A dog with spots plays in the snow.

Stan Stirs the Stew

Blend the **s** and **t** sounds to say the beginning sound in **Stan**, **stir**, and **stew**. Circle the pictures that begin with the same sound as **Stan**, **stir**, and **stew**.

car

star

stove

vest

stamp

Crossword Fun

Match the pictures to the words in the list. Fill in the puzzle.

stove   stop   spill   spoon   sled

Across

1.

2.

3.

Down

1.

2.

STOP

Sweet Swap

Blend the **s** and **w** sounds to say the beginning sound in **sweet** and **swap**. Circle the pictures that begin with the same sound as **sweet** and **swap**.

sweater

swan

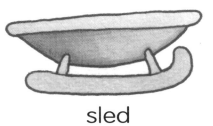

sled

swing

clown

Steve Sweeps and Swims

Read the sentences. Draw a line from
each sentence to its matching picture.

Steve swims with a swan.

Steve sweeps stones.

Steve swallows a sweet.

Crossword Fun

Match the pictures to the words in the list. Fill in the puzzle.

sweep   stone   spoon   swim   stem

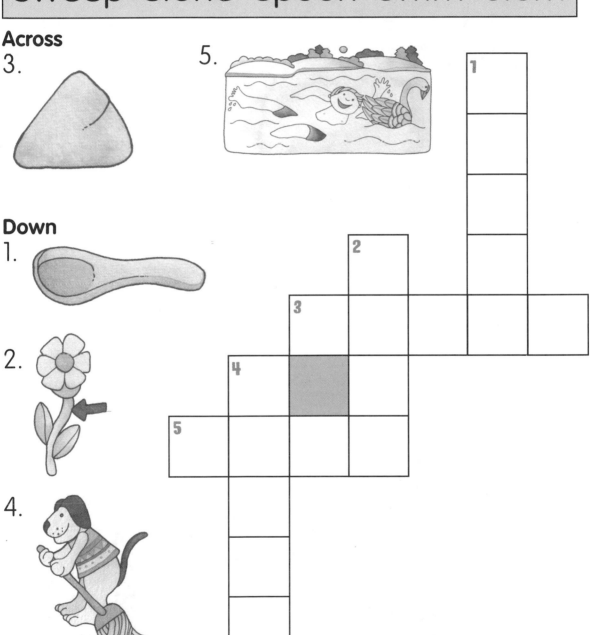

Across

3.

5.

Down

1.

2.

4.

3-2-1 Blast Off!

Blend the **b** and **l** sounds to say the beginning sound in **blast**. Circle the pictures that begin with the same sound as **blast**.

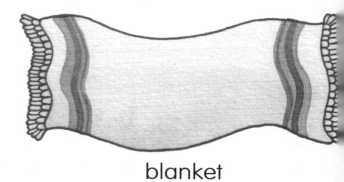

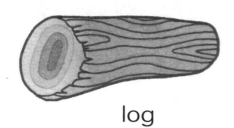

log

blanket

block

blow

box

The Cliff Climbing Club

Blend the **c** and **l** sounds to say the beginning sound in **cliff**, **climb**, and **club**. Circle the pictures that begin with the same sound as **cliff**, **climb**, and **club**.

clam

clown

clock

lamp

can

A Clown for the Class

Read the sentences. Draw a line from
each sentence to its matching picture.

The clever clown blows balloons.

The clown wears silly clothes.

The class claps for the clown.

A Flea on a Float

Blend the **f** and **l** sounds to say the beginning sound in **flea** and **float**. Circle the pictures that begin with the same sound as **flea** and **float**.

flower

lips

flag

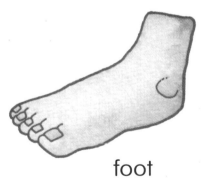

foot

flute

Crossword Fun

Match the pictures to the words in the list. Fill in the puzzle.

block   clam   flute   flat   flame   blade

Across

1.

4.

6.

Down

2.

3.

5.

Glen Is Glad!

Blend the **g** and **l** sounds to say the beginning sound in **Glen** and **glad**. Circle the pictures that begin with the same sound as **Glen** and **glad**.

goat

glass

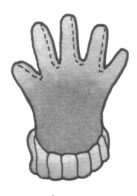

glove

lamb

globe

Match Game

Draw a line from each word to its matching picture.

flute

glass

glue

flag

flame

A Place to Play

Blend the **p** and **l** sounds to say the beginning sound in **place** and **play**.
Circle the pictures that begin with the same sound as **place** and **play**.

playground

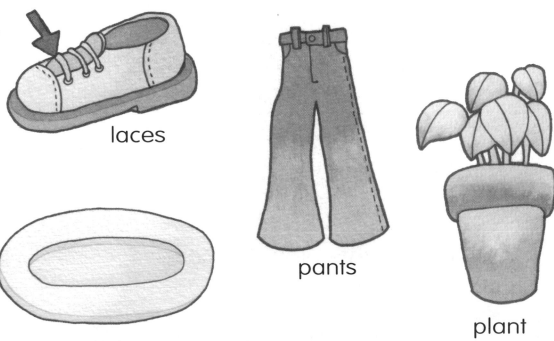

laces

pants

plant

plate

Patty and Lulu

Read the sentences. Draw a line from each sentence to its matching picture.

Patty eats a plum on a plate.

Lulu plants plenty of seeds.

Patty and Lulu play on the playground.

Fill in the Blanks

Finish the sentences. Use words from the word list.

Look at the pictures for clues.

clock	plate	glass

I eat from a _____.

I drink from a _____.

I use a _____ to tell time.

Crossword Fun

Match the pictures to the words in the list. Fill in the puzzle.

float flag plum plus plant

Across

1.

2.

3.

Down

1.

2.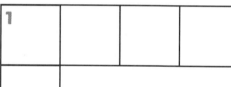

The Bride and Broom?

Blend the **b** and **r** sounds to say the beginning sound in **bride** and **broom**. Circle the pictures that begin with the same sound as **bride** and **broom**.

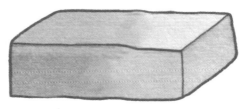

brick

bush

brush

rain

bridge

Cross the Creek Carefully

Blend the **c** and **r** sounds to say the beginning sound in **cross** and **creek**. Circle the pictures that begin with the same sound as **cross** and **creek**.

crown

swing

crayon

plant

crib

Cross the Bridge

Read the sentences. Draw a line from
each sentence to its matching picture.

This brick has a crack.

A crab creeps and crawls in the creek.

The bride will cross the bridge.

Look, Drew Can Drive!

Blend the **d** and **r** sounds to say the beginning sound in **Drew** and **drive**. Circle the pictures that begin with the same sound as **Drew** and **drive**.

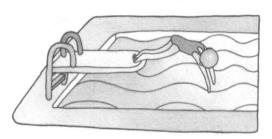

dive

dragon

frog

duck

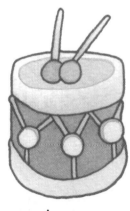

drum

Crossword Fun

Match the pictures to the words in the list. Fill in the puzzle.

drum dress brick crab bride

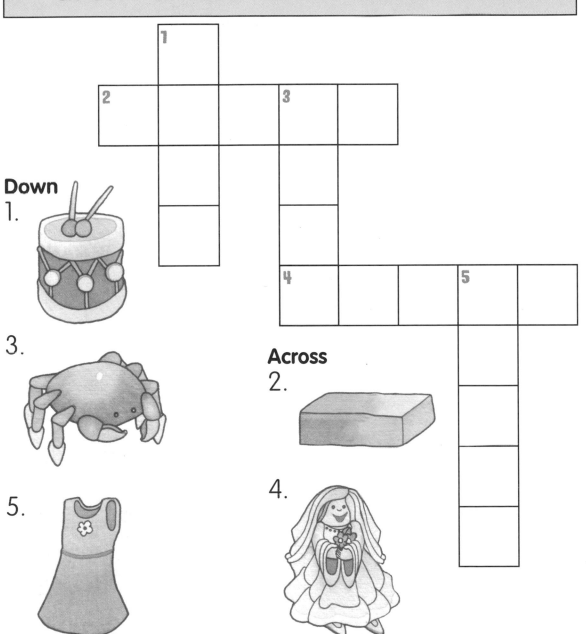

Down

1.

3.

5.

Across

2.

4.

Deep Freeze

Blend the **f** and **r** sounds to say the beginning sound in **freeze**. Circle the pictures that begin with the same sound as **freeze**.

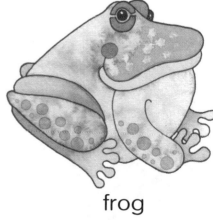

French fries

fruit

rake

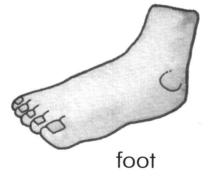

foot

frog

Match Game

Draw a line from each word to its matching picture.

fruit

drum

frame

frog

dress

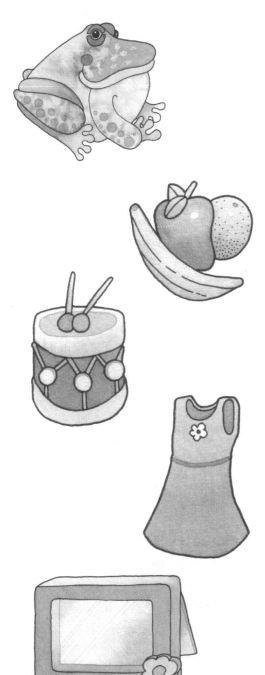

Great Grade, Greg!

Blend the **g** and **r** sounds to say the beginning sound in **grade** and **Greg**. Circle the pictures that begin with the same sound as **grade** and **Greg**.

grasshopper

rock

girl

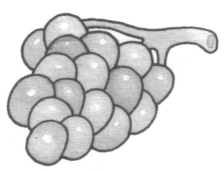

grass

grapes

Oh, So Pretty!

Blend the **p** and **r** sounds to say the beginning sound in **pretty**. Circle the pictures that begin with the same sound as **pretty**.

pipe

bathrobe

present

princess

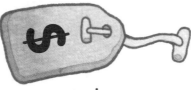

price

All About Greg

Read the sentences. Draw a line from each sentence to its matching picture.

Greg eats a grape in the grass.

Greg grabs the prize.

Greg grins.

Crossword Fun

Match the pictures to the words in the list. Fill in the puzzle.

fruit frame prince price grin

Across

4.

5.

Down

1.

2.

3.

Trick or Treat?

Blend the **t** and **r** sounds to say the beginning sound in **trick** and **treat**. Circle the pictures that begin with the same sound as **trick** and **treat**.

truck

rain

triangle

tire

tree

Terrific Trina

Read the sentences. Draw a line from
each sentence to its matching picture.

Trina trains her dog to do tricks.

Trina travels on a train.

Trina takes a trip in a truck.

Fill in the Blanks

Finish the sentences. Use words from the word list.
Look at the pictures for clues.

tree   grass   dress

They play in the _____.

He sits under a _____.

She wears a _____.

Crossword Fun

Match the pictures to the words in the list. Fill in the puzzle.

tree crack broom bridge truck

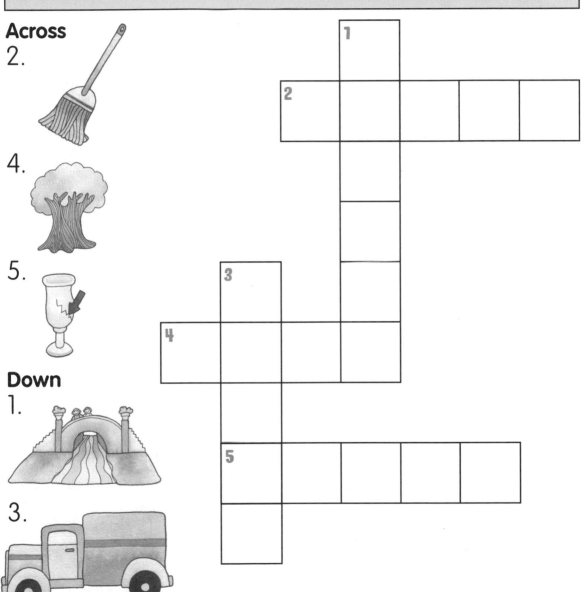

Across
2.

4.

5.

Down
1.

3.

May I have a hug?

Ask Nicely!

Blend the **s** and **k** sounds to say the ending sound in **ask**. Circle the pictures that end with the same sound as **ask**.

padlock

desk

rock

tusk

mask

Take a Rest, Pest

Blend the **s** and **t** sounds to say the ending sound in **rest** and **pest**. Circle the pictures that end with the same sound as **rest** and **pest**.

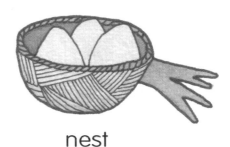

nest

toast

vest

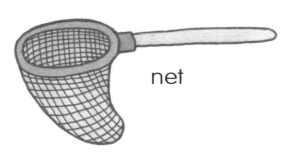

net

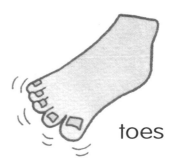

toes

How Do You Eat Toast?

Read the sentences. Draw a line from
each sentence to its matching picture.

I eat toast at a desk.

I eat toast in a vest.

I eat toast in a nest.

Crossword Fun

Match the pictures to the words in the list. Fill in the puzzle.

dust toast nest desk mask

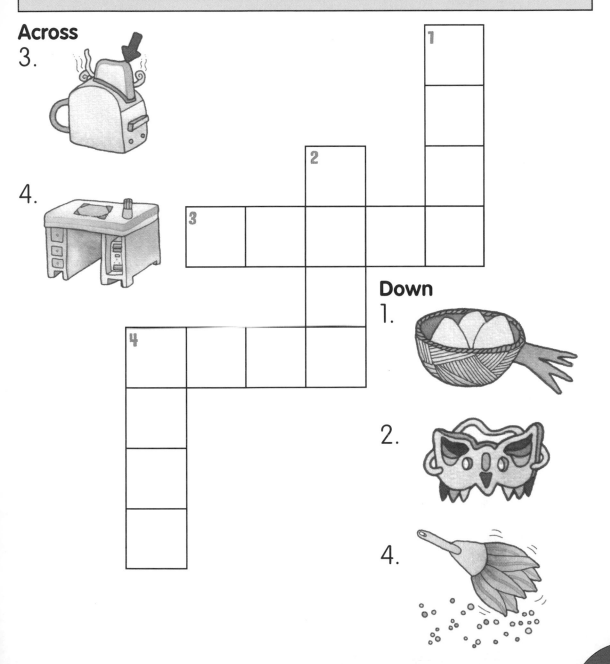

Across

3.

4.

Down

1.

2.

4.

The Old Wolf Went for a Walk

At the end of some words, the letter **l** comes before another consonant. To say these words, blend the **l** sound with the following consonant.

Circle the picture that ends with the same sound as **old**.

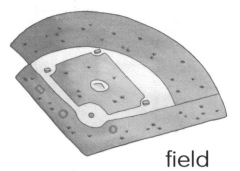

field

ball

Circle the picture that ends with the same sound as **elf**.

wolf

bell

Circle the picture that ends with the same sound as **walk**.

duck

milk

An Elf by Himself

Read the sentences. Draw a line from each sentence to its matching picture.

The milk is cold.

The chalk is on the sidewalk.

The elf is all by himself.

Crossword Fun

Match the pictures to the words in the list. Fill in the puzzle.

milk cold hold shelf chalk

Across

2.

3.

4.

Down

1.

3.

Don't Melt!

Blend the **l** and **t** sounds to say the ending sound in **melt**. Circle the pictures that end with the same sound as **melt**.

quilt

bell

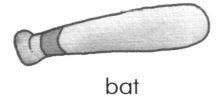

bat

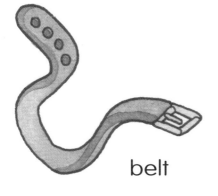

belt

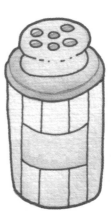

salt

Lift It

Blend the **f** and **t** sounds to say the ending sound in **lift**. Circle the pictures that end with the same sound as **lift**.

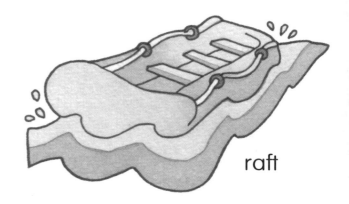

raft

mitt

leaf

gift

give

Match Game

Draw a line from each word to its matching picture.

gift

salt

raft

belt

quilt

Crossword Fun

Match the pictures to the words in the list. Fill in the puzzle.

melt lift quilt belt gift

Across

1.

4.

5.

Down

2.

3.

Jump over the Bump

Blend the **m** and **p** sounds to say the ending sound in **jump** and **bump**. Circle the pictures that end with the same sound as **jump** and **bump**.

stamp

stop

cap

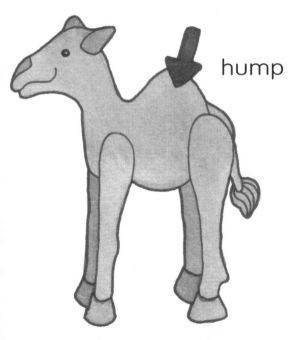

hump

lamp

Jump and Stomp

Read the sentences. Draw a line from each sentence to its matching picture.

Don't jump with a lamp.

This camp is damp.

The horse chomps the hay and stomps his feet.

Crossword Fun

Match the pictures to the words in the list. Fill in the puzzle.

lamp	damp	pump	hump	jump

Across

3.

4.

5.

Down

1.

2.

A Band in the Sand

Blend the **n** and **d** sounds to say the ending sound in **band**.
Circle the pictures that end with the same sound as **band**.

hand

pond

can

fan

sand

Kent Went on a Hunt

Blend the **n** and **t** sounds to say the ending sound in **Kent**, **went**, and **hunt**. Circle the pictures that end with the same sound as **Kent**, **went**, and **hunt**.

ant

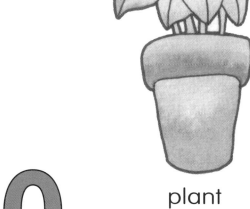

plant

10
ten

net

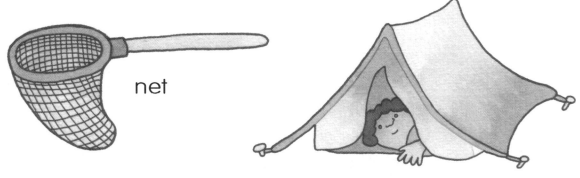

tent

An Ant, a Tent, and a Magic Wand

Read the sentences. Draw a line from each sentence to its matching picture

Look out for ants in the sand.

He spent a cent at the fruit stand.

She has a wand in her hand.

Crossword Fun

Match the pictures to the words in the list. Fill in the puzzle.

hand   band   tent   sand   ant

Across

2.

5.

3.

Down

1.

4.

Good work,

_____
(Name)

!

Give Yourself an A+!
Now you know your
consonant blends!